My Parents Are Getting a Divorce... I Wonder What Will Happen to Me.

An interactive discussion book
for children ages 4–12.

Written by

Karen Kaye, LMHC
and her daughter, **Hara Wachholder**, LMHC

DEDICATION

I kept my promise.

This is for you, Mom and Dad.

To my daughter, Hara...

You inspire me.

To the children.

Copyright © 2019 by Karen Kaye, Hara Wachholder

Interior illustrations and design by Samuel Wilson
Cover and interior layout by Masha Shubin | Inkwater.com

ISBN 978-1-0879-2671-1

1 3 5 7 9 10 8 6 4 2

INTRODUCTION

Dear Parents, Therapists, School/Guidance Counselors, Teachers, Mediators, and Lawyers,

My daughter Hara and I come to this project from a first-hand experiential viewpoint. My husband left me when my daughter was 18 months old. The shock and shame sent me into a black hole for three months, but then I realized I had a job to do. I wanted to teach my daughter that when someone leaves you, don't allow that person to own you the rest of your life. I stopped looking at my ex-husband's new life and created a pretty great world for my daughter and myself that is continuing to amaze me to this day. I guess my success angered my ex-husband, because 10 years later he went for custody of our child, which is when the idea for this book began. I made a promise to God that if I was able to keep my precious child, I would write a book to help other single parents raise emotionally whole, well-balanced children, no matter what their circumstances. Your circumstances surrounding the divorce may be different from mine, but the ultimate goal is to lessen the impact of your divorce on your children.

As a therapist in private practice for 37 years, I witness parents being so focused on the "fight" between each other that they forget to raise their children, thus allowing their children to "drown" in the middle of what should be their divorce – not their children's divorce.

To any parent who chooses to read a book like this with their children:

I congratulate you for wanting more for you and your children! You will make a difference with the following tips in mind. Your biggest gift to give your children is to work on yourself and your emotions (preferably with a qualified professional). Your reactions to the divorce will directly affect your children's feelings.

While parents are referred to as "Mom and Dad," this book was written for all of the unique families that are looking to help themselves and their children during the tough time of divorce. Please utilize this book with the "titles" that best suit the needs of your family.

My suggestion is to first read this book alone to explore your own feelings and answer the questions for yourself. You will need to be grounded and neutral in order to interact with your children when discussing this book. Be prepared to hear ideas and feelings from your children that you will not necessarily agree with, nor want to hear. If you are on "overload," feeling hurt or angry, this may be the time to focus on your emotions before you can adequately be available for your children. You can take this book (as a tool) to a qualified professional for some of the topics you want to address, until you are ready to work with your children to better your communication and your relationship.

Any adult (parent, therapist, school/guidance counselor, teacher, mediator, and lawyer) working with children and their feelings must provide a safe, non-biased environment for the children to explore their feelings, without repercussion. Please refrain from leading questions and misinterpretations. You must see yourselves as a "blank canvas" that children can draw upon, using their own words, feelings, and in their own time.

Please note this book is not a "quick fix." It is meant to provide a beginning to the lengthy process of healing, and is not meant to replace good, quality counseling. With that being said, I recommend that this book be utilized to record your child's first thoughts and feelings regarding the divorce. Children can continue to explore their thoughts and feelings in a separate notebook/journal to see how things have changed, as well as to address any other areas of concern. A continuous update (every 3 months) should be made throughout the first few years.

I highly recommend that both parents seek counseling for their individual needs and to learn how to co-parent their children. Parents who decide to seek therapy for their children need to screen each professionals' framework and choose therapists that are child-oriented as well as focus on divorce as a specialty. It is crucial to help children deal with difficult and confusing feelings now, which will result in better-adjusted, healthy adults in the future.

For those of you who reside within the State of Florida and prefer to arrange a session with me, you can contact me via karenkayecares@bellsouth.net

All the best,
Karen Kaye, LMHC

HARA'S LETTER TO THE CHILDREN

My parents got divorced when I was young. I know how hard it is to understand what is going on. When my dad left, I felt like he didn't want me anymore. He found a new wife and new kids. I was sad and confused. I did not know what I did wrong. Instead of telling my mom how I felt, I kept all of my feelings inside of me. I became angry all of the time and cried a lot. My mom saw that I was hurting and bought me a journal. I drew pictures and wrote anything that I was thinking or feeling. A great place for you to share your thoughts and feelings would be on the "My Own Space" pages of this book. Even if you do not feel comfortable talking to someone else, it is important to tell your truth (at least to yourself) to feel better.

As I have gotten older, I see that the divorce was not my fault. I was just a kid and I did nothing wrong. I still write in my journal because it is my safe place to let all of my feelings out. After I write everything down, I take a deep breath and feel a little better. It is good to know that you can help yourself feel better and that you are not the only kid with parents that are divorced or divorcing. It is also important to know that you are not alone, and it is okay to ask for help as well as to share how you are feeling. I hope this book helps you feel better.

Love,
Hara

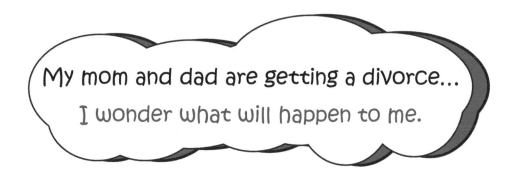

My mom and dad are getting a divorce...
I wonder what will happen to me.

Mom and Dad may not end up living together
but I know they will still think about me...

Divorce is when Mom and Dad are no longer married,
but they are still my parents who take care of me.

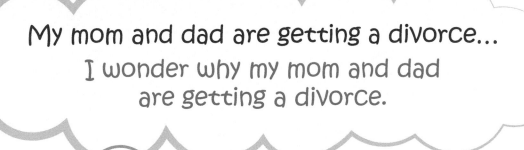

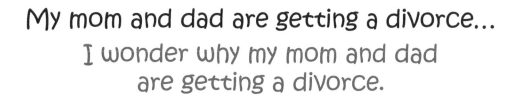

My mom and dad are getting a divorce...
I wonder why my mom and dad
are getting a divorce.

Did something happen?
Why did they make this decision?
Will Mom and Dad be happy now?
Will Mom and Dad get along now?

My Own Space by: _____

(My name goes here)

I understand that my parents are getting a divorce because:

I don't understand why my parents are getting a divorce because:

My other questions for my mom and dad are:

All I Know is... I'm Still Me!

My mom and dad are getting a divorce...
I wonder if I can get my parents back together.

My mom and dad are getting a divorce...

I wonder if I can get my parents back together.

Do I want them to stay together?

If I am good, will Mom and
Dad get back together?

Is it wrong if I want them to stay together?

Is it wrong if I want them to leave each other?

If they won't get back together, will
my parents be able to get along?

My Own Space by: _____
                        (My name goes here)

I do believe my parents will stay together because:

I do not believe my parents will stay together because:

My feelings about my parents not staying together are:

My other questions for my mom and dad are:

All I Know is...
I'm Still Me!

My mom and dad are getting a divorce...

I wonder if it is okay for me to love
both my mom and my dad.

Will Mom get mad at me for loving Dad?

Will Dad get mad at me for loving Mom?

Whose side do I pick?

Is it okay for me to love them both?

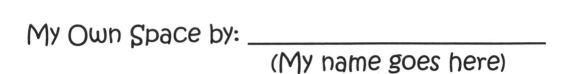

My Own Space by: _____
                               (My name goes here)

I know it is okay to love my mom and dad because:

My feelings about loving both my mom and dad are:

My other questions for my mom and dad are:

All I know is...
I'm Still Me!

My mom and dad are getting a divorce...

I wonder what will change for me.

Changes can be scary or maybe changes just take time getting used to.

What do I think will change?

Where will I live?

Who will I live with?

What about my brothers and sisters?

Where will I go to school?

When will I see my mom?

When will I see my dad?

What about my pets?

When will I see my friends?

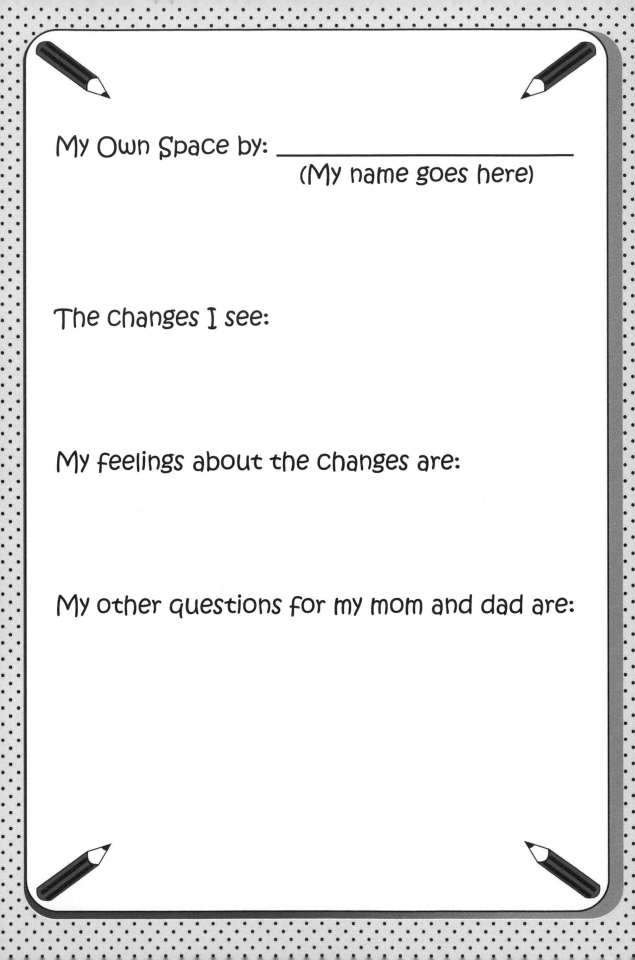

My Own Space by: _____
                        (My name goes here)

The changes I see:

My feelings about the changes are:

My other questions for my mom and dad are:

All I know is...
I'm Still Me!

My mom and dad are getting a divorce...

I wonder what will stay the same.

I will still look like me.

I will still sound like me.

My parents care about me
and I care about them.

I still care about me.

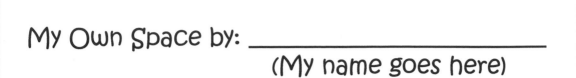

My Own Space by: _____
                        (My name goes here)

The things I know that will stay the same are:

My feelings about the things that will stay the same are:

My other questions for my mom and dad are:

All I know is...
I'm Still Me!

My mom and dad are getting a divorce...
Do I see my parents acting differently?

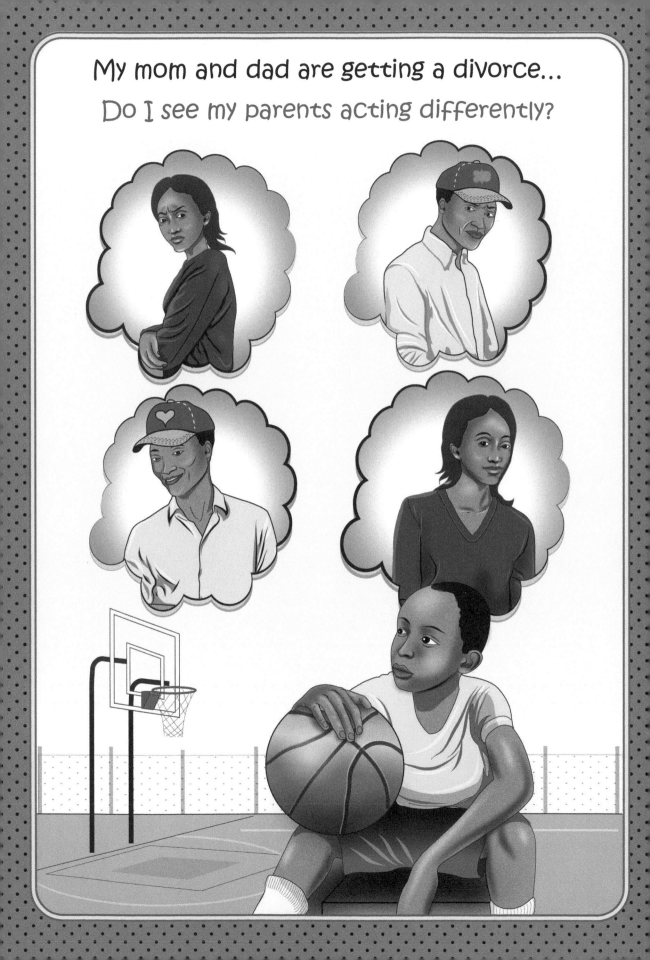

My mom and dad are getting a divorce...

Do I see my parents acting differently?

Is Mom or Dad looking sad?

Is Mom or Dad looking worried?

Is Mom or Dad looking angry?

Is Mom or Dad looking happy?

My Own Space by: _____
                          (My name goes here)

The feelings that I see in my parents are:

My feelings about the way my parents look are:

My other questions for my mom and dad are:

All I know is...
I'm Still Me!

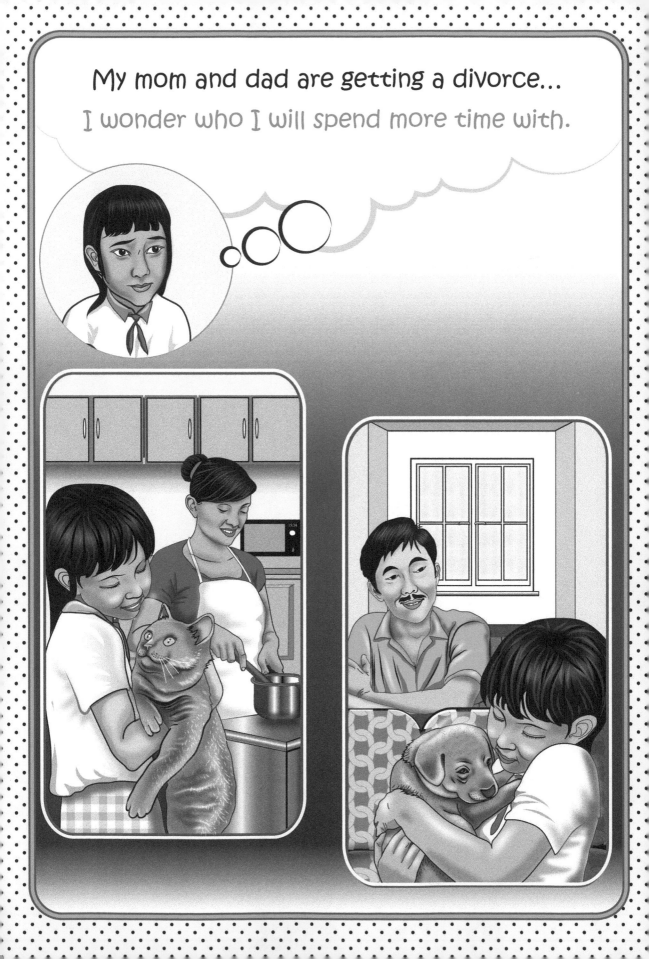

My mom and dad are getting a divorce...

I wonder who I will spend more time with.

When will I spend time with Mom?

When will I spend time with Dad?

When will I spend time with my
brothers and sisters?

When will I spend time with my other relatives?
(grandparents, aunts, uncles, cousins)

When will I spend time with my friends?

When will I spend time with my pets?

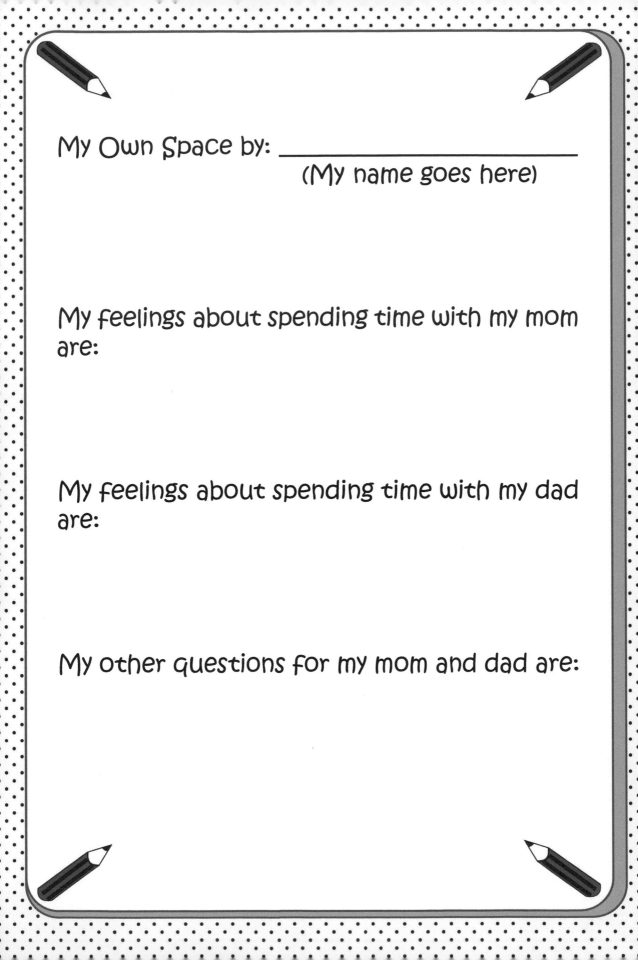

My Own Space by: _____
(My name goes here)

My feelings about spending time with my mom are:

My feelings about spending time with my dad are:

My other questions for my mom and dad are:

All I know is... I'm Still Me!

My mom and dad are getting a divorce...

I wonder if I will still see my friends.

If I am living in a different place,
when will I see my friends?

When I am with Mom, when
will I see my friends?

When I am with Dad, when
will I see my friends?

Will I have to make new friends?

Are any of my friends' parents
divorced or getting a divorce?

Will my friends treat me differently?

My Own Space by: _____
(My name goes here)

When I see my friends, I feel:

When I can't see my friends, I feel:

My other questions for my mom and dad are:

All I know is... I'm Still Me!

My mom and dad are getting a divorce...
I wonder how I feel.

My mom and dad are getting a divorce...

I wonder how I feel.

When do I feel scared?

When do I feel mad?

When do I feel sad?

When do I feel lonely?

When do I feel happy?

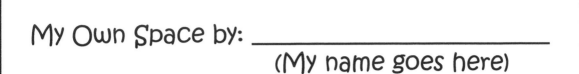

My Own Space by: _____
                              (My name goes here)

All of my different feelings are:

Expressing my different feelings to someone who cares can help me feel better because:

My other questions for my mom and dad are:

All I know is... I'm Still Me!

My mom and dad are getting a divorce...
I wonder how I can get my feelings out.

My mom and dad are getting a divorce...

I wonder how I can get my feelings out.

I wonder if I will feel better if:

I talk to my mom?

I talk to my dad?

I draw a picture?

I hit my pillow on the bed?

I scream into my pillow?

I cry?

I write my feelings in a journal?

I talk to my friends?

I talk to my teacher,
school/guidance counselor, and/or therapist?

What are other ways that I can
help myself feel better?

My Own Space by: _____
(My name goes here)

I feel good when:

I feel bad when:

My other questions for my mom and dad are:

All I know is...
I'm Still Me!

My mom and dad are getting a divorce...
I wonder when I will feel better.

My mom and dad are getting a divorce...

I wonder when I will feel better.

I know that getting my feelings out may hurt at first, but it can help me feel better.

I know it will take time to feel better.

I will have to give myself more love and hugs.

I will keep drawing, writing, and/or talking about my feelings.

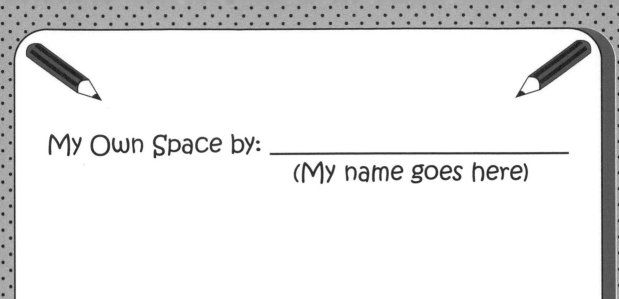

My Own Space by: _____

(My name goes here)

I will know that I am feeling better when:

My other questions for my mom and dad are:

All I know is...
I'm Still Me!

My mom and dad are getting a divorce...
BUT I'M STILL ME!

Drawing of Me goes here:

Remember...you are not alone!

This is Mom and Dad's divorce, and
you didn't make it happen.

You are more important than your parents' divorce.

PRAISE FOR THIS BOOK

My Parents Are Getting A Divorce interactive discussion book is a valuable and thoughtful resource for divorcing parents and their children. The mother/daughter co-author introduction provides a clear understanding of how parents, counselors and other professionals can use this workbook as a tool for more useful and effective communication with children of divorce. As founder of the Child-Centered Divorce Network, I appreciate the simplicity as well as value of each question being asked. Children from 4 to 12 are invited to think about and answer these questions and also come up with questions of their own. These promptings enable parents and professionals to get deeper insights into challenges, fears or insecurities children are coping with that they may not be expressing. Used as designed, this beautifully illustrated discussion book can help children understand what is happening to them in the present as well as how life may look for them well into the future. It also stimulates deeper family discussions which is always of value for every parent.

Rosalind Sedacca, CDC
Founder, Child-Centered Divorce Network
Author: *How Do I Tell The Kids About The Divorce*

CPSIA information can be obtained
at www.ICGtesting.com
Printed in the USA
LVHW071645110321
681235LV00015B/1993

9 781087 926711